Copyright © 2018 Anthony Andrade

All rights reserved. No part of this publication may be reproduced or distributed in any form or by any means, or stored in a database or retrieval system, without the prior written permission of the author, except where permitted by law.

Legal & Disclaimer

The information contained in this book is not designed to replace or take the place of any form of medication or professional medical advice. The information in this book has been provided for educational and entertainment purposes only.

The information contained in this book has been compiled from sources deemed reliable, and it is accurate to the best of the Author's knowledge. However, the Author cannot guarantee its accuracy and validity so cannot be held liable for any errors or omissions. Changes are periodically made to this book. You must consult your doctor or get professional medical advice before using any of the suggested remedies, techniques, or information in this book.

Upon using the information contained in this book, you agree to hold harmless the Author from and against any damages, costs and expenses, including any legal fees, potentially resulting from the application of any of the information provided by this guide. This disclaimer applies to any damages or injury caused by the use and application, whether directly or indirectly, of any advice or information presented, whether for breach of contract, tort, negligence, personal injury, criminal intent, or under any other cause of action.

You agree to accept all the risks of using the information presented inside this book. You need to consult a professional medical practitioner in order to ensure you are both able & healthy enough to participate in this program.

Contents

Introduction 3

Chapter 1: Survey of the Problem of Procrastination 7

Chapter 2: Practical Strategies to Stop Procrastinating 11

    Strategy 1: Narrow your Focus.. 11

    Strategy 2: Set Personal Deadlines 12

    Strategy 3: Stop Striving for Perfection...................................... 14

Chapter 3: Strategies and Techniques for Focus 15

    Strategy 4: Walking Without Thinking 15

    Strategy 5: Minimize Distractions 16

    Strategy 6: The Self-Scan, or "GTD"....................................... 17

    Strategy 7: Create a Visual Map of Your Time 18

Chapter 4: Getting to Work 20

    Strategy 8: Clear Your Work Space... 20

    Strategy 9: Stop Multitasking 21

    Strategy 10: Mindfulness and Getting to Work 22

    Strategy 11: Give Yourself Rewards 24

Conclusion 25

Introduction

The problem of procrastination seems to be such a feature of life that it has found some form of acceptance. We hardly think of it as a problem at all and certainly not one that can be mended. We are all well aware of the student who leaves everything for the last minute. This has become such a common theme that jokes are often made about it—the perennial problem of the student who just will not get things done is a cliché. The workplace is also plagued with the problem of procrastination. There always seems to be that one person who is lagging behind everyone else and who must scramble in the end to get things finished. Specific tasks that are tedious and unexciting always get done last—things that no one wants to do that therefore get left until the final hour. These are the common-place features of procrastination, and everyone is familiar with these things on some level.

We have all heard of Leonardo Da Vinci and most of us know about his famous painting titled 'Mona Lisa', possibly one of the most well-known works of art in human history. What if I told you it took Da Vinci 16 years to complete it? What is more, many of Da Vinci's works remain unfinished to this day—he just never got around to finishing them. Leonardo Da Vinci took his time to do anything, and most of the projects he started, he never finished. He was so bad for not completing his ventures that one of his benefactors had to threaten bankruptcy in order to compel him to finish a work that they had commissioned. Well known authors such as Franz Kafka and Victor Hugo—despite producing many of the most celebrated works of literature—were also procrastinators who left works unfinished and left their contemporaries exasperated with their work habits. Even the Dalai Lama, one of the most recognized and celebrated men in the world today, is known for his habitual procrastination. It would seem the problem plagues even some of the greatest minds in history.

It would be easy at this point to shrug our shoulders and say "If it works for the greats, it works for me." Many people will even claim that procrastinating puts them in the right frame of mind to get things done; that they work best under the pressure they create for themselves when they put things off. For most of us procrastinating is a source of anxiety, but one we know we will have to deal with at some point. Thus, we procrastinate about doing something about procrastinating. We accept the problem as an unfortunate evil in life, but procrastination causes problems. Our health suffers from the undo stress, our jobs suffer because of wasted time, and those close to us suffer because we just do not get things done the way we need to.

Another thing to consider about procrastination is that it is downright expensive. Procrastinating and wasting time has an actual monetary cost, and this number can be staggering. One study showed that the amount of revenue lost due to interruptions from social media and similar electronic distractions was on the order of $650 billion a year! Chats, IMs, and social media notifications... the cost of time wasted for emails and texts is estimated to be as much as $700 billion a year. And if you think these kinds of figures apply only to corporate and business losses you would be wrong. This same study showed that the average American loses approximately $400 a year simply because they procrastinate on filing their taxes. That is four hundred dollars from an individual's pocket, wasted just because of procrastination.

The problem of procrastination is well documented and wide spread. It is not just a nuisance to us personally; it costs us money and leads to unnecessary stress, anxiety, and frustration. As we can see, this problem seems to cross all lines, from household chores to the highest endeavors we can imagine.

One would think that a problem so common and so well documented would have been properly addressed and "cured" by now, that the modern disciplines of psychology and neuroscience would have found the root of this evil and stamped it out. The truth is that the psychology of the problem of procrastination is so common-place, the conclusions of the experts is that it cannot exactly be cured, and we can only find ways of dealing with it. Procrastination is a mental and emotional pest that often times will not go away, and since the underlying causes are numerous and complex, an overall solution becomes impossible to find.

Clinical psychologists have linked the existence of procrastination primarily with anxiety; both being a cause and effect of the other. When we are confronted with specific kinds of tasks, most notably tasks which are either unfamiliar (and therefore provoke fear of the unknown), or unpleasant (and provoke negative associations), this triggers anxiety and we have a natural instinct to move away from such stimuli. By recoiling from the unpleasant or anxiety inducing task, we can become anxious at not completing it. A cycle gets set in motion and can become difficult to break. These same experts have shown that procrastination of this type is largely associated with people who demonstrate low self-worth and self-esteem problems, and people tend to have adopted a pattern of "learned helplessness" as a result of different underlying issues.

A more common cause of procrastination is quite simply impulsiveness and a break-down of our self-control. The issues described above (along with perfectionism at the other end of the spectrum) tend to be associated with some real psychological problems, but most of us procrastinate simply because we allow our own self-control to get away from us and we act on impulses rather than reasoned and planned behavior. It is easy to do—we see a project or task that we don't like, or one we simply do not feel like doing, and we impulsively decide to put it off.

This last set of causes and behaviors are quite simple and are therefore just as simply unlearned. What we require is a set of specific strategies which will help us circumvent the impulsive reactions which lead us to procrastinate in the first place. So, the good news is that where the problem is simple, so is the solution.

The strategies we will cover are simple things anyone can do without the help of any special equipment, electronic devices, or specialists. These are practical strategies to beat procrastination which we can apply immediately. These strategies have been proven to give positive results. If we remember that procrastination is the gap between intention and action, we can begin to see that it is fairly easy to overcome. Procrastination is little more than a misfire between what we really need or want to do and our ability to act on it. The strategies in this book are all about bringing us to the crucial moment of taking action. From simple thought exercises, to physical arrangements, to more complex mental practices, this book will lead you through eleven powerful and simple strategies to beat procrastination.

Enjoy it!

Chapter 1

Survey of the Problem of Procrastination

When I was in graduate school I was always given as many as twelve weeks to write my research papers. I had what amounted to three months to generate ideas, do the research, and write a twenty page paper. Inevitably, term after term, I would wait until the last week to start the paper. I would stay awake for days on end; I would stress and worry, and wear myself down to finally get the paper finished and handed in on time. Every term I would swear I would start early and every term I would procrastinate until the final week and go through the same self-inflicted torture. What is more, I knew many others who did the same thing—some who even waited until the final three days. Over the years I have encountered numerous people, some of them quite successful, who habitually procrastinate on important matters of all kinds.

Waiting until the last minute seems to be a practice as old as humanity itself. Denunciations and discussions of procrastination go back at least as far as classical antiquity, in which we find the philosopher Hesiod in the 5th century BCE who warned against the evils of putting things off. The question as to why we do this is just as ancient; even more complex is how the problem is viewed. While some argue that procrastination actually benefits those who claim to work best under pressure, others believe that procrastination is detrimental in all of its forms.

One way to begin looking at this issue is to differentiate procrastination properly from other forms of mental activity that may not actually involve physically doing something, but nevertheless involve engaging the mind toward a task. There are those who do spend time pondering problems and mentally planning how to go about completing them, and because these are activities of the mind, they can easily appear to be forms of procrastination, when in fact these are often instrumental in accomplishing something. Experts define the true procrastinator as someone who quite literally comes to a task with a full absence of progress—they have done nothing to even mentally begin the work. While those who mentally plan and prepare for a task may well struggle to complete it as they approach the deadline, the true procrastinator does nothing at all until the last minute. What is more, the notion that anyone works well under this type of pressure has been dispelled by researchers who have shown that the true procrastinator simply suffers more from the anxiety and stress of running late for a deadline and their work suffers from the rush to completion. There is no benefit for the person who procrastinates nor is there any measurable quality to the work completed at the last minute.

Going back to my graduate school experience, I can see that while I did wait until the final week to begin writing my paper, I was not a true procrastinator. I actually spent weeks preparing to write it; I had been taking notes, reading, and planning throughout the term. And I had a full set of themes mapped out, even though I had left myself little more than a week to do the writing. My colleagues who really did wait until the final days of the term were positively harried in their attempts to finish their work. They generally received poor marks on their papers, and many of them never finished graduate school. The notion that some of us just work better under pressure does not seem to hold up under scientific, and even anecdotal, scrutiny.

We are left with the question, then, as to why we do this. Why do so many people procrastinate when it is well known that putting things off makes us miserable and results in shoddy work? One answer is that some people lack a structure for their projects or tasks. This is especially true in our time because of the freedom so many people have now in how they get their work done. Unlike times past, in which people generally were on a rigid time-clock and under the immediate scrutiny of a supervisor, much of the work that characterizes the contemporary economy is done in non-traditional work places, and often times at home. For some, the lack of a rigid structure causes them to lose the focus necessary to stay on task. It seems safe to say that students have always dealt with this problem, as schools at any level will provide a great deal of structure, but once they are free to do the work outside of the classroom or to sit and watch television (or any other distraction from working), many students lose the focus they need to stick with important tasks. The employee who labors outside of the traditional work environment as well as the student shares this obstacle. Both find themselves without any of the traditional organization which compels one to stick to a task, and they inevitably start to put things off— in some cases, get nothing done at all.

Much of this seems obvious, but it is worth noting that any unpleasant task will inevitably become a source of procrastination. This seems to be human nature, and it is likely that nearly all of us are guilty of it. Obviously, anything we really do not want to do will get put off for as long as we can get away with it, but then, there are those who recognize that a task is unpleasant, and, for the same reasons that many of us will procrastinate, these people will prioritize these tasks in order to get them out of the way. Even though this cause of procrastination seems obvious, it has its exceptions, which further complicates how to approach the problem more generally. Why do some people attack the unpleasant task, while others put it off until everything that made it unpleasant in the first place is now compounded by being late?

Moreover, the causes of procrastination all come with their own individual solutions, and these solutions will be dealt with in this book. Suffice it to say for the moment that procrastination generally leads to poor performance and bad work. The tasks that require attention suffer for being delayed, and though we can always find exceptions to this, the fact remains true enough across the board— those who procrastinate suffer for their poor work habits and derive no real benefit from putting things off, and the time spent being lazy or even relaxing is spoiled by the amount of time spent caught up in anxiety and stress over a task which requires attention. What we need are some real strategies for dealing with the problem of procrastination. We require some concrete measures any of us can take which will lead us toward more productive uses of our time, so that our down time is spent relaxing rather than worrying about what we have not finished.

Chapter 2

Practical Strategies to Stop Procrastinating

One of the main reasons people fall into the trap of procrastination is simple anxiety. This anxiety stems from the fear of failure and the anticipation of catastrophes. Strange as it may sound, psychologists have found that many people, prior to even beginning a project or task, imagine the worst possible outcomes and anticipate failure. What this amounts to is allowing the imagination to anticipate the worst and then losing all sense of proportion with respect to what actually can be done. In short, people lose focus—they begin to think about everything but the task at hand. There are some techniques and strategies designed to maintain focus as we approach a project that we can use to combat this.

Since procrastination is a problem which all of us deal with on some level, the keys to eliminating procrastination for most people are actually quite simple. Most of us need a few easy strategies to get us focused and working and we are good to get things done. This chapter focuses on these simple but indispensable strategies.

Strategy 1: Narrow your Focus - Doing one small thing is better than doing nothing

Almost any job consists of a series of small steps. Too often we approach a job, project, or task with the entire finished product in mind. This leads to an overall block toward how to begin. When we are looking at a project with every essential feature of it in the fore of our minds, we often become frozen in place, and so this can become a major source of procrastination. When we feel like there is too much to work with, we cannot work with anything. The key is to simply narrow our focus. Break the task down into small, easily understandable and achievable tasks, and work at one thing at a time.

The issue of focus is a problem for the chronic procrastinator. For these people, the "big picture" is always the primary focus. They see the entire project, every step involved and the finished product all at once, and they are unable to begin anything. They ultimately convince themselves that the job is just too big for them. One expert counsels people to follow this simple program of narrowing your focus.

There is a category of procrastinators who become paralyzed at the thought of beginning a project due what is called performance anxiety. These types of people immediately anticipate the worst case scenarios as described above, but also fear success as much as failure. This may seem like a paradox, but people who deal with performance anxiety are actually afraid of successfully completing a task or project. More specifically, these people fear the responsibility of being successful. They are afraid that success itself brings about more responsibility for future success. Those who live with performance anxiety are among the worst procrastinators, since not only do they put off doing the task, they are actually afraid of beginning and even more afraid of finishing it. The first recommendation of psychologists and counselors for these types of people is to narrow their focus. Something as simple as approaching a larger project with an eye toward only the smallest features of it will allow someone with performance anxiety to begin the task. Narrowing our focus leads us from one small piece of the big picture to another until the entire project is accomplished.

Strategy 2: Set Personal Deadlines - Writing down deadlines to finish large tasks one step at a time

We trick ourselves into thinking we will always have time to get the job done. In this way, we trick ourselves into thinking there is always plenty of time to begin the job, thus, we procrastinate. We put off getting started until a deadline is upon us, at which point the anxiety and stress takes over and we are in danger of terminal procrastination in which we do nothing at all. By setting personal deadlines—small due dates meant only for ourselves—we can achieve the goals we set above, and we avoid the pitfall of waiting until the last minute to get started.

Suggested methods for setting personal deadlines come from freelance workers who need to map out their work on their own. They suggest writing these deadlines down and keeping them in a place that is always visible. Treat your own deadlines the way a boss would treat them. Once the deadline is set, view it as something that comes from a supervisor. Finally, include someone else in the deadline; if another person who has a stake in your project or work knows about it, you are no longer only answerable to yourself. This person may not be a supervisor who can dole out punishment, but he or she will be someone to whom you are accountable. This alone motivates most people. These methods have worked for those who absolutely cannot afford to procrastinate.

Another method for setting deadlines is to create a timeline toward completing the task. A timeline takes the idea of writing down deadlines to a more complex level. In this method, you draw out a line which will take you from start to finish. Fill in the line with set goals, and with specific times to reach them. In this, you will be breaking your project into smaller mini-projects and following the timeline rather than looking at the entire picture. This combines the process of breaking the job into smaller, more manageable pieces, with the idea of setting personal deadlines. If you draw out or write down the timeline and follow it, you won't spend time thinking about how big the job is. You will be focused on completing small tasks, one at a time, and once you reach the end of the timeline, you will find the entire project finished.

There are apps available which can help with setting and maintaining a personal schedule complete with deadlines and notifications. Many of these apps have electronic notification systems which remind you of what is coming up and what you need to accomplish. While electronic devices and cell phones are often the main source of distractions which cause us to procrastinate, they can also be used to beat procrastinating. In this case, the poison is also the cure. Electronic scheduling apps can be broken down into small increments so that you are able to schedule things over the course of, say, a work week. But you can also set these schedules so that the myriad tasks of a single day can also be arranged, complete with mini-deadlines. You can prioritize work that needs to be attended to in any order you require. Again, the notification features are extremely helpful—you can actually set your phone up to nag you into doing what you need to do!

Strategy 3: Stop Striving for Perfection - Done is better than perfect

This is a trap many of us fall into. We all want things done well, but doing a good job is not the same thing as perfection. The pressure that comes with this ideal of perfection can be crippling. Remember that done is better than perfect, and it is always better to get something accomplished than to do nothing at all. When we get caught up in seeing perfect results, we introduce stress into a task we have not even begun. The immediate tendency for most people is to see the perfect results as unattainable and then stop before they start; writers will tell you it is better to edit a flawed page than to work with a blank page. If we get started and get something done, we can always go back and polish the results after the fact. We cannot revise and polish anything if nothing is accomplished. Avoid the problem of perfection from the start.

It may be helpful to know that perfectionism is not exactly the virtuous ideal many of us think it to be. Perfectionism is not really a function of a disciplined need to have things done perfectly, really, the psychology of perfectionism is in fact an expression of fear. Low self-worth and a fear of being found lacking in life generally fuel the need to make things perfect. This is a defense mechanism against criticism which many people find humiliating. If we let go of this idea that we absolutely must make things perfect or not do them at all, we will free ourselves. We will "give ourselves permission" if you will, to not only make mistakes and fix them, but also to accomplish things. In short, if we free ourselves form the false aspiration of perfectionism, we are free to get things done and do them well.

Chapter 3

Strategies and Techniques for Focus

To struggle with procrastination from time to time seems to be just about universal. Some of us already have methods to kick-start our work day or to give us a boost toward accomplishing a task, but for others, procrastination becomes something that overwhelms them. These people can become frozen just at the thought of what they have to do, and so are unable to act. The more people procrastinate, the more the anxiety and stress of not working mires them in procrastination. What most of us need are some simple and practical strategies to get us moving.

Strategy 4: Walking Without Thinking - The science of walking and focusing

For many procrastinators the problem seems to be a mental block of sorts. People become paralyzed by their own thoughts as ideas mix with anxiety. This dangerous combination produces even more fear, which of course leads to an even more firmly entrenched state of procrastination. This may seem counter-intuitive but many experts actually suggest taking a walk without thinking about anything at all. Taking a walk would make sense to many people, yet, the idea of not thinking about anything runs counter to what we are after; surely we need to at least consider the work before us? The obvious benefit of a walk would be to turn the ideals and issues around in your mind until you get to a reasonable place to begin working. Walking without thinking advocates the opposite approach—get away from the task and the work space, and simply wander. Let your mind relax and avoid thoughts which directly relate to the task or project. What many experts have found is by doing this we release the mind entirely, including the stumbling blocks to getting started. This process achieves two things; the mind gets a little exercise—a warm up, for getting down to business, and you also refresh your mindset. In much the same way that working the same muscle will eventually exhaust that muscle, working your mind on one specific project can wear out your thinking. Taking a short walk and getting away from the issue allows you to relax and come to the task or project with a fresh set of ideas and thoughts. It is important to remember that this should be a short walk—strenuous exertion will eventually work against you.

Walking without thinking is essentially a form of meditation. Just as meditation generally works to clear the mind of clutter by slowing down our physical movements and regulating things like breathing, walking without thinking enables us to physically change what we are doing and clear our minds of thoughts which have become defeating. Let the mind simply wander without trying to regulate or consciously direct, and relax into being present. After taking a short walk and clearing the mind, most people are able re-approach a task. They see a project which had become overwhelming in a new and fresh light and they are able to at least begin the work. And as we have already noted, a task begun soon becomes a task completed.

Strategy 5: Minimize Distractions - Clearing clutter

This seems obvious, but cutting out distractions is an absolutely essential strategy to stop procrastinating. Turn the television off. Put away electronic devices which are not essential to the task at hand. If you must listen to music, do not listen to music which compels you to sing, dance, get lost in reveries, and so on. This strategy can be made to complement the designated work environment, since the space you set aside for work can be made free of these kinds of distractions. Situate yourself far from the television and other entertainment systems which can pull you from the task at hand. Do not clutter your work space with objects, books, magazines, and other things that are too easy to pick up and divert your attention.

As you consider removing distractions, remember that work time is not time to socialize. If you are prone to texting or talking on the phone, you should consider turning it off, or at least putting it out of reach so that it is not such an immediate temptation. Take account of all emails and text messages before you get down to work— this way, you will have a hard time convincing yourself that there is something crucial waiting for you on your device and you will be less likely to be tempted to check.

For those who simply cannot put their phones down, there are apps available online—some free, some at minimal cost—which actually block some features of electronic interruption. These are technical apps which allow you to block, for example, Facebook notifications for a specific period of time. If you think you may need something this advanced, it is worth doing a little research to see if these things are for you. For many of us, the process of setting up our notifications is too cumbersome and a simple app may be just the thing we need.

One more method to avoid distractions is to change your work space. This will not work for everyone, but for those whose projects are mobile, it can be a magnificent idea to take your work someplace away from home. One expert suggests taking your work to a place that is free of all your familiar diversions, one that is not filled with things that take your attention away from your work. This follows for finding places that inspire us to work, and we should remember that a space which inspired us before may not keep doing so. If we are prone to get off task at home or if we find a specific work space to be uninspiring, a change of scenery might just be the thing we need. It is a familiar sight to see people working in cafés. Many people take their work to places like this because it frees them of all the familiar distractions at home, school, or even the office. Changing the place where you work could be the thing to beat your procrastination.

Strategy 6: The Self-Scan, or "GTD"—A method of Self-Regulation

One important approach to have before we begin a task is to have work strategies in place. One of the major reasons we fall into procrastination is that we have no real plan of attack when it comes to approaching anything. There are a number of strategies for beginning the job, but one good one which stands out is called "GTD - Getting Things Done". Like so many of the strategies for avoiding procrastination, it seems obvious until we begin to approach a job, and then we begin procrastinating instead of working.

GTD breaks things down into steps, beginning with a series of questions. Simply put, GTD asks why we are doing this and how we are going to get it done. Beginning with these simple questions, we begin to see both the importance of the task at hand and we get a preliminary set of ideas of what will be necessary to get it done. The next step is to plan the job—write down the steps necessary to begin the task and then prioritize them. In the planning stage, we visualize the task, define the purpose of the task, and then begin brainstorming and organizing. Remember, these are simple things to do before you even begin to take on the job you have before you.

A sub-section of GTD is called the 2-Minute Rule. This is a very simple, but tremendously effective way, in beating procrastination. Whenever we face a project or job, we mentally (or on paper) sort out the basic parts of the job. We quickly decide where and how to begin. Procrastination intervenes precisely at this moment, as we are mentally sorting through what to do first, that impulse to simply sit back down and wait, or to do something else that seems more fun or interesting steps in, and we shy away from our task. The 2-Minute Rule tells us to stop thinking and impulsively do anything that takes about two minutes to accomplish. It does not matter how important or unimportant it is; just start doing it and spend the full two minutes doing it. What experts have found is by attacking any task that appears fast and easy, we jump-start our commitment to doing the entire task. This simple trick has been proven to work wonders.

Strategy 7: Create a Visual Map of Your Time

This is exactly what it sounds like. Not everyone works best with a list—some people are more spatially oriented and a visual map works better for them. Rather than looking at a written list, the map provides a picture that arranges the parts of a project in space rather than in sequence, drawing out the time you have allotted to accomplish your goals. Making it colorful and visually appealing will help. You should be able to look at it and instantly see a clear picture of each step of your work day or project; mapping this out according to things which are most time sensitive. Leave the aspects of the project which qualify as finishing touches in less immediate colors (the colors themselves do not matter. It is up to you to determine which will best alert your attention). The goal is to have a clear picture of the project or task and each step necessary to complete it. By having something clearly visualized, the task and each small step becomes less abstract and therefore less subject to the negative effects of a wandering mind. The fear of failure and catastrophe becomes less daunting when we see small tasks instead of a single big task which can overwhelm us before we start.

Chapter 4

Getting to Work

Now you have worked through some of these strategies—you have chosen those which help you focus and which eliminate distraction. You have even possibly used some of the strategies designed to help yourself into being in a "get-things-done" mentality. Now it is time to being the work. This is a critical moment, because it is at this point that procrastination can work its way back in and divert you from the goal you want to accomplish. Once we sit down to do the task, things need to be in place in such a way as to facilitate working rather than goofing off or becoming distracted.

Strategy 8: Clear Your Work Space

It is absolutely essential that the space you set aside to work in remains a work space and not a place for diversions and junk. This space should not be cluttered or filled with things which can lead you off task. I know that if my desk is scattered with junk, I get caught up in it, even if all I am doing is moving it around. As soon as I, or most anyone else, get diverted by clutter, we become prone to falling into all of the procrastination issues we have already covered.

There is an entire cognitive system behind the problem of clutter, and it is intimately tied to procrastinating. Without getting bogged down in this, it is enough to point out that experts have shown that working in a cluttered environment is not only an expression of disorganization, but that it produces disorganization. Not being properly organized is a fundamental cause of procrastination. When we have our thoughts going in too many directions, we end up becoming unable to act. If our work environment is operating in the same way, it will prevent us from taking the actions we need to take to complete the project. Cleaning up and organizing the work space is an indispensable strategy to beat distraction and therefor procrastination.

Order your work space in such a way as to align your tasks with your list, timeline, or deadlines. Take a few minutes to set the work out before you in a way that follows the order you have already created on paper. If you are working at a desk, have the pieces of the project lined up in front of you in the order of completion. This way, as you finish one small task, the next one is there for you to move on to. If the work is not desk work, set the pieces of the task out in such a way that they follow a logical order. Both of these suggestions will allow you to finish one thing and easily move on to the next without getting sidelined on something which leads you to start procrastinating again. Much of this is simple but if we take the time to order and clear space around us, we find things simply getting done without having to think about it.

Strategy 9: Stop Multitasking

This may seem counter to conventional wisdom, but the whole idea of multitasking sounds good in theory while in reality it is really a recipe for defeat. When we attempt to do multiple things at one time, more often than not we end up accomplishing nothing. Juggling multiple projects at the same time cause confusion, and confusion causes stress and anxiety—two of the principle reasons why we procrastinate in the first place. Though the idea of multitasking can be appealing—we would all love to get everything finished at the same time and in half the time—we do not really see the kind of results commonly associated with multitasking in a successful light. As a strategy to stop procrastinating, it is always more beneficial to focus on one project at a time.

There was a time when it was believed that multitasking was the answer to managing a large set of tasks and getting them finished. The business ideals of recent decades saw multitasking as a way to maximize productivity in workers; the belief was that we could train people to handle multiple tasks if we ordered those tasks in the proper way. All of this has been shown to be a fallacy. Psychologists have demonstrated that the human mind is not capable of actually focusing on more than one thing at a time—it just is simply not possible. Multitasking actually often leads to confusion and anxiety. Having multiple things going on at the same time can simply overwhelm our attention and our stamina in such a way that we become unable to do anything at all, comparable to trying to listen to multiple conversations at the same time; all we end up hearing is noise and we become aggravated. Multitasking has this effect on the brain and our reaction to it is the same. We become frustrated and this will inevitably lead to doing nothing at all. We are liable to end up with something that feels a lot like justified procrastination.

If you approach a task or project with the belief that you can handle multiple features of the work at the same time, you are setting yourself up for failure. That fear of failure will be confirmed and you will have handed yourself a list of reasons to procrastinate. It is best to just jettison the myth of multitasking from the outset. It just does not work.

Strategy 10: Mindfulness and Getting to Work

This is an advanced strategy, but it is one that has a lot of evidence behind it as a meaningful practice for avoiding procrastination. In order to approach this we need to re-visit why we procrastinate in the first place. There is at least one simple reason for procrastination: we simply do not want to do what needs to be done. Psychologists describe this a being part of emotion regulation. We seek what is called "short-term mood repair" and turn our attention away from the sources of our negative emotions. We simply avoid things which cause us stress, and this avoidance is manifested as procrastination. In order to work with negative feelings in a more comprehensive fashion, we need to learn techniques which help us manage these moods and emotions in relation to those things which we cannot avoid, such as jobs and projects which require our attention. Mindfulness training and practices work well for this problem.

To properly manage negative emotions we need a method which is effective for regulating feelings more generally. Mindfulness offers a comprehensive tool for managing emotions. It works to create a present-moment awareness, which is precisely the thing we need to avoid procrastinating. Mindfulness is based on ideas which train the mind to be completely in the present—in the moment, as it were—rather than allowing the mind to wander into future outcomes which have not even happened yet. This also keeps our minds from wandering into memories of the past and negative associations we may have with the present task we seek to work with; such memories and associations conjure negative feelings toward a moment and thus we avoid the projects of the present.

One of the key features of mindfulness is learning a non-judgmental acceptance of the present moment, complete with all of the things which define it. By practicing mindfulness, we learn to simply allow the present moment to exist on its own. We take the present moment for exactly what it is, without any speculations or judgments as to the meaning of it. All of our reactions to this are derived only from the conditions before us.

In order to achieve the mindfulness state of being, counselors and psychologists recommend a period of quiet meditation before we approach a task or project. If we take just a little time to sit quietly and, rather than focusing on anything in particular, allow all thoughts and feelings to pass through the mind with as little internal reflection as possible, we become present. During this type of meditation we will experience the negative feelings and thoughts we associate with the project we have before us, but rather than ruminating on that negativity associated with the project, we allow ourselves to feel these emotions without trying to control them. This is to say that the negative thoughts and feelings will come to us, but we will not allow ourselves to bring judgments and conclusions to bear on these feelings. Mindfulness training suggests that by meditating on things in this way, the negative emotions we seek to avoid will occur and pass through the present moment without taking hold of our attention and leading us toward procrastination habits we acquired to deal with them in the first place.

Mindfulness may well be one of the more advanced strategies for dealing with and avoiding procrastination, but it is a proven method and one which is recommended by psychologists.

Mindfulness may seem extreme in comparison to some of the other more straight-forward strategies detailed so far, but the reality is it takes no more time to practice a meditative mindfulness strategy than it does to organize and make lists. Experts recommend just a few minutes of quiet meditation, which allows people to work with the emotions and negative associations they may have toward getting certain jobs done. Short periods of mindfulness meditation have been shown to produce real results in avoiding the trap of procrastination.

Strategy 11: Give Yourself Rewards

Giving yourself treats can seem selfish or self-indulgent, when in fact psychologists explain that treating and rewarding yourself is an important part of self-regard, which is vastly different than being selfish. Learning new habits and changing the way we do things, including learning how to beat procrastination, is a crucial feature of self-regard, which consists of learning to value yourself for the right reasons. Self-regard based on being responsible and being able to get things done on time is central to a healthy sense of self.

I put this final strategy to beat procrastination at the end because the reward belongs at the end, when everything is finished. All this amounts to, is learning to be good to yourself for getting the job done. Before you begin, even before you decide how to begin, promise yourself a reward for getting things accomplished; you hold out a promise to yourself that once everything is done, there is a treat waiting for you at the end. Obviously, this is not an excuse to blow all of your money on big-ticket items, although, depending on the project you set out to finish, a big-ticket item might be warranted. But more simply, just tell yourself that once this job is done, you get to indulge in something special: an expensive beer or glass of wine, something decadent to eat—it doesn't really matter. What matters is that as you buckle down to get the job done, where there is a reward waiting for you at the finish line.

Conclusion

The problem of procrastination impacts us all—whether we are procrastinating ourselves, or doing our best to wait patiently on a procrastinator, the problem of not starting or not finishing a job impacts everyone. As we have seen, the issue reaches just about any strata of life. Great artists and writers and everyone else, it would seem, are prone to putting things off until the last minute—even the great Leonardo Da Vinci was subject to threats in order to get started on things, and even then he left much undone.

We can also see that the solution to beating procrastination is often quite simple and requires us, most of all, to simply acknowledge that we are procrastinating. Just admitting to ourselves that this is what we are doing seems to be the first step toward a solution. Most of these strategies for beating procrastination first require a step that involves taking responsibility for what we have to do and then implementing a strategy to get it done. Even the most complex solutions, mindfulness meditation for example, depend on a self-acknowledgment of procrastinating.

I think we can see that both the problem and the solutions all have a psychology which underlies them. It is easy to say that the chronic procrastinator is simply irresponsible, but that does little to help when a job needs done. In fact, there can be some fairly serious issues which attend chronic procrastination and some of the strategies in this book should hopefully help with those.

There are eleven strategies here which will help you beat procrastination. You should feel free to experiment with them to decide which will work best for you. None of them are exclusive either—anyone could combine multiple strategies to optimize their ability to accomplish goals large and small. Taking the strategy to make lists and narrow focus can easily lead directly into something more complex; find the magic combination that makes you more productive.

For the average person— one who finds themselves with a job before them and little motivation to get started—these strategies should get them moving and getting to work. That there is scientific evidence behind these strategies should give you confidence that they are effective; some of these strategies have been put to use in actual work environments to great success. The cost to business due to procrastinating is steep. Businesses have much at stake in seeing that their work-force has powerful methods to become efficient at completing tasks.

Finally, none of these strategies require much of an investment to use. The use of more sophisticated methods such as apps is an option, but you should be able to take these eleven strategies and effortlessly begin putting them to work in your daily life. By way of a little more confidence in these strategies, there is recent research on both psychology and neuroscience behind procrastinating. These types of studies, as you may expect, draw out vast complexities which underpin the problem. In the final analysis, most of what these researchers suggest is outlined in this book. All we need are these 11 strategies to beat procrastination.

--- Anthony Andrade.

www.ingramcontent.com/pod-product-compliance
Lightning Source LLC
Chambersburg PA
CBHW071001220526
45471CB00007B/3128